The Ven. Maha Sthavira
Sangharakshita

Other books by the same Author:

MESSENGERS FROM TIBET AND OTHER POEMS

A SURVEY OF BUDDHISM

ANAGARIKA DHARMAPALA: A BIOGRAPHICAL SKETCH

THE THREE JEWELS: AN INTRODUCTION TO BUDDHISM

THE ESSENCE OF ZEN

CROSSING THE STREAM

THE PATH OF THE INNER LIFE

THE THOUSAND-PETALLED LOTUS: AN ENGLISH BUDDHIST IN INDIA

THE ENDLESSLY FASCINATING CRY

BUDDHISM AND BLASPHEMY

HUMAN ENLIGHTENMENT

THE RELIGION OF ART

the essence of Zen

Five Talks by

The Ven. Maha Sthavira

Sangharakshita

Windhorse Publications

136 Renfield Street, Glasgow G2 3AU

1985

Printed by Antony Rowe Ltd, Chippenham

Originally published in 1973 by
Friends of the Western Buddhist Order
Windhorse Press edition published 1976
Windhorse Publications edition 1983
Reprinted 1985

Contents

Publishers Note

As this is a popular rather than a scholarly work, diacritical marks have been omitted from Sanskrit words, as well as from Indian proper names.

Preface

After spending twenty years in the East, mainly in India, I returned to England in August 1964 at the invitation of The English Sangha Trust, and was for two years Incumbent of the Hampstead Buddhist Vihara, London. During this period I delivered at the Vihara upwards of a hundred lectures on various aspects of Buddhism, including five talks on 'The Essence of Zen'.

The present work is a transcription of these talks, which were given towards the end of 1965. Though the passage from the spoken to the written word has inevitably resulted in a certain amount of condensation, I have tried to resist the temptation of recasting the substance of these talks in more 'literary' form. In this way, I hope, I have not only remained closer to the Heart of Ch'an but avoided the obvious inconsistency of producing yet another "book on Zen". Despite the fact that you are now reading with your eyes rather than listening with your ears, in the following pages I am still just talking . . . I wonder if you can hear me.

Freathy Bay,
Cornwall.
26th April, 1973.

A special transmission outside the Scriptures;
No dependence on words or letters;
Direct pointing to the mind (of man);
Seeing into one's own nature and realizing
Buddhahood.

First Talk

Introduction

Zen is one of the best known and most important forms of Buddhism, and for a long time I have been wondering whether to speak on the subject. I was aware that, in venturing to speak on Zen, I would be treading on very dangerous ground. Some people, indeed, might regard me as a trespasser on their own special preserve. However, after pondering the matter for some time I decided to take my courage in both hands and speak on Zen. There will, therefore, be a series of five talks on 'The Essence of Zen', of which the first talk in the series, the one I am giving today, will be of an introductory nature.

My reluctance to speak on Zen was certainly not due to any feeling of disrespect towards this form of Buddhism. I have in fact the greatest admiration for Zen. Along with the Maha Mudra and Ati Yoga teachings of Tibet it represents, in my opinion, the peak of Buddhist spirituality. My reluctance was due rather to an awareness of the extreme difficulty of doing justice to the subject. I was also aware of the numerous misunderstandings surrounding Zen, some at least of which would have to be dispelled before Zen itself could be approached. However, having given series of lectures on the Theravada and Mahayana schools, as well as on Tibetan Buddhism – not to mention an odd lecture on Shin, – I eventually decided that, for the sake of completeness at least, I ought to overcome my reluctance and speak on Zen too.

A few words about my personal connection with Zen might be of interest here. At the age of sixteen I happened to read *The Diamond Sutra* and *The Sutra of Wei Lang* (as *The Platform Scripture* was then called) and immediately had the intuitive perception that here was the absolute truth which, far from being new to me, was what I had really known and accepted all the time. Like many others, I also read the writings of Dr. D.T. Suzuki and his imitators. Suzuki's own words on Zen, with their combination of erudition, intellectual brilliance, and spiritual profundity, impressed me deeply, and I have returned to them for inspiration throughout my Buddhist life. For more than twenty years, mainly in the East, I studied and practised forms of Buddhism other than Zen. In particular, I practised meditation according to Theravada methods and according to the Tantric traditions of the Tibetan Buddhist schools. These studies and practices, and the spiritual experiences to which they led, deepened my understanding and appreciation of Zen. This will seem strange only to those who tend to regard the different forms of Buddhism as so many mutually exclusive entities each of which has to be approached independently and as it were *de novo*. Far from being mutually exclusive, all the schools of Buddhism, despite their immense diversity, have a great deal of ground in common, so that to experience the truth of any one of them is to some extent at least to grasp the inner meaning and significance of all the others. All are concerned, ultimately, with the attainment of Enlightenment. Having known the truth of Buddhism by practising, for example, a form of Tibetan Buddhism, it is therefore possible to understand and appreciate the Theravada or the Jodo Shin Shu. Knowledge of the whole includes knowledge of the parts. In order to understand the spirit of Zen one does not always have to read books on 'Zen Buddhism', or stay at a monastery labelled 'Zen Monastery', or even practise

'Zen meditation' – much less still learn Japanese or sit on cushions of a particular size and shape.

However, had that been all, had my connection with Zen been limited to my experience of *The Diamond Sutra* and *The Sutra of Wei Lang,* my reading of Suzuki's works, and my general understanding of Buddhism, it is very doubtful whether I should have ventured to speak on the subject. But fortunately there was one more link. Before returning to England in 1964 I was in contact with a very remarkable man. This was a lay Buddhist hermit living on the outskirts of Kalimpong in two small rooms which he has now not left for at least fifteen or sixteen years. From five in the morning until five in the afternoon he sat, and I am sure still sits, in meditation, with a short break for lunch. Visitors are allowed only in the evening, by appointment. For several years I saw him regularly, usually on Saturday evenings. Besides possessing a thorough knowledge of the canonical literature of Buddhism he was, I soon found, an advanced practitioner of the Vajrayana, which he had studied in Eastern Tibet, as well as of Zen or, as I ought to say, since he was Chinese, of Ch'an. He was moreover a prolific writer, publishing numerous books on Tantric Buddhism and Zen, though he allowed himself only half an hour a day for literary work. Despite the fact that he refused to act as a guru, and accepted no disciples, in the course of talks and discussions I was able to learn a great deal from him. In particular I was able to imbibe the spirit of Zen in greater measure. Had it not been for this contact I probably would not have felt able to speak to you about Zen at all.

Now you may have noticed that so far as these talks are concerned I have arrived at the subject of Zen as it were schoolwise. That is to say, having given courses of lectures on the Theravada, on the Mahayana, on Tibetan Buddhism, and so on, I finally decided to give, for the sake of completeness, a series of talks on Zen. This brings us to an extremely important point, a point directly affecting the nature of the Buddhist movement not only in this country but throughout the Western world. Buddhism has a long history. It has flourished in the East for 2500 years, and during this time, in India, China, Japan, Tibet and elsewhere, numerous sects and schools have sprung up. Nobody knows exactly how many of them there are – or were, for some are extinct. Probably there are several hundred still in existence. These schools present a picture, or pattern, of unity in diversity, and diversity in unity. All aim at the attainment of Enlightenment, or Buddhahood. At the same time they approach it in a number of ways and from many points of view. They are either predominantly rationalist or predominantly mystical, inclined to activism or quietism, situating their teaching in a historical or mythological context, and so on. These schools, or at any rate some of the most important of them, are now in process of being introduced into the West. Partly on account of the reasons already adduced, and partly through being associated with different national cultures, they at first present, to the Western student, a spectacle of unmitigated difference, not to say disharmony. But we should not allow ourselves to be mislead by appearances. Despite their apparent differences, even mutual opposition, we should study and learn to appreciate them all, thus making ourselves acquainted, as far as possible, with the whole vast range of Buddhist thought and practice. Only in this way will it be possible for us to obtain a balanced picture of Buddhism. Otherwise, we might commit the mistake of identifying Buddhism with one or another of its expressions, maintaining that this, and this alone, was the true embodiment of the Buddha's teaching. Such a course would be unfortunate as it would mean, in effect, adopting an attitude of sectarian exclusiveness which, though unfortunately characteristic of most forms of Christianity until recent times, is quite foreign to the spirit of Buddhism.

In this place we do not identify ourselves exclusively with any particular school. Therefore, having dealt with so many other forms of Buddhism, it was inevitable that sooner or later we should get round to Zen. This synoptic kind of approach is, of course, a very difficult, even confusing, one to follow. It demands ability to discriminate what is essential from what is inessential in Buddhism. It demands objectivity and power of judgment, as well as a considerable amount of hard study. Most of us shrink from the effort involved. After all, it is so easy, in comparison, to "take up" the form of Buddhism to which we are most strongly attracted, to identify ourselves wholeheartedly with it, to derive emotional satisfaction, perhaps, from proclaiming this, and this alone, to be the true Dharma, and all the other forms travesties, misrepresentations, and corruptions! But the temptation must be resisted. We must remember that, as Buddhists, we take refuge in the Dharma, not in the teachings of this or that particular school. Our line of spiritual practice may, indeed must, be specialized, at least to some extent: we either recite the Nembutsu, *or* practise mindfulness of breathing *or* visualize a mandala of Buddhas, Bodhisattvas and other deities. But our general approach, our overall attitude, to Buddhism, should be as broad as possible. Indeed, it should be universal.

In this connection I remember my experience at the Buddhist Society's Summer School in 1964, shortly after my return from India. There were lectures and classes on the Theravada, Mahayana, Zen and Tibetan Buddhism. Going from one meeting to another, as most of them did, some of the newcomers very quickly became disheartened and confused. Sometimes it seemed as though Buddhism was severely rational, strictly ascetic, and rather dry; sometimes as though it was warm, mystical and ethically permissive. In one class they would be told to *think*; in another, to use their intuition. One speaker would sternly exhort them to rely on their own efforts for salvation; immediately afterwards, perhaps, another would invite them to rely solely on the compassion of Amitabha, the Buddha of Infinite Light, Who in ages long gone by had already graciously accomplished their salvation. No wonder the newcomers were bewildered! Some, indeed, were heard to remark that they had learned a lot about the Mahayana, the Theravada, and various other schools, but where, they asked, was Buddhism? When were they going to hear about that? For most of them however, light eventually dawned, and by the end of the week they had begun to realize that, despite their contradictions, all schools aimed at Enlightenment, all were concerned with one or another aspect of the same transcendental Reality.

We have had the same type of experience in our Speakers' Class. On one occasion four people, two men and two women, were asked to speak for twenty minutes each simply on 'Buddhism'. Though the subject was the same, they produced four completely different talks. In fact, the talks could hardly have been more dissimilar. To begin with, the two men's approach to the subject was noticeably more intellectual; that of the women, more intuitive. While one speaker gave a systematic exposition of the Four Truths and the Noble Eightfold Path, another devoted the whole of her talk to the subject of meditation. One of the four included a detailed account of the life of the Buddha. Another did not mention the Buddha at all. At the same time, despite their different approaches, all four talks were recognizably about the same thing – Buddhism. It was as though all, while inevitably falling wide of the central point of the incommunicable essence of Buddhism, in aiming at it drew, at different angles, lines which between them demarcated an area, or described a figure, within which Buddhism could be found and experienced. However comprehensive and objective we try to make them, our approaches to Buddhism are inevitably limited and conditioned, in short, one-sided. As my experience at the Summer School, and in the Speakers' Class, illustrates, one way in which we can transcend this onesidedness is by juxtaposing contradictory formulations of Buddhism in such a manner that we not only experience their contradictoriness but realize that they are equally valid expressions of a spiritual experience that for ever eludes the logical categories of the discriminative mind. This is one of the benefits to be derived from a comprehensive study of different schools of Buddhism. We should not be afraid of contradictions. 'A foolish consistency', said Emerson, 'is the hobgoblin of little minds'.

On the psychological plane Buddhism attaches great importance to harmony and balance. Human nature has a number of different aspects, intellectual and emotional, active and contemplative, and so on, and justice must be done to them all. In the spiritual as in the secular life, all must be cultivated and developed, and a perfect equilibrium maintained. This is illustrated by the doctrine of the Five Spiritual Faculties, one of the most ancient and important of the 'numerical lists' in which from an early date, the Buddha's teaching was preserved. The Five Spiritual Faculties are Faith *(shraddha)*, Wisdom *(prajna)*, Vigour *(virya)*, Concentration *(samadhi)*, and Mindfulness *(smriti)*. Faith, representing the emotional and devotional aspect of the spiritual life, must be balanced by Wisdom, otherwise it runs riot in religious hysteria, persecution mania, fanaticism, and intolerance. On the other hand Wisdom, which stands for the intellectual, better cognitive or gnostic, aspect, must be balanced by Faith, without which it speedily degenerates into hair-splitting scholasticism. Vigour, or the active, kinetic aspect of the spiritual life, must be balanced by Concentration, representing the introspective, contemplative counter-tendency, without which Vigour is either animal high spirits or neurotic restlessness, and Concentration itself by Vigour, divorced from which Concentration is aimless reverie, morbid introspection, or neurotic withdrawal. Mindfulness, the remaining faculty, being by its very nature incapable of going to extremes – one can't have too much mindfulness – requires no counterbalancing faculty to hold it in check. Mindfulness it is, indeed, that keeps Faith and Wisdom, and Vigour and Concentration, in a state of equilibrium. 'Mindfulness is always useful', the Buddha once declared.

Besides being one of the schools of Buddhism Zen is, more specifically, also one of the schools of the Mahayana – the second of the three great stages of historical development into which Indian Buddhism traditionally falls. In the Mahayana four major schools, or types of approach, can be distinguished, and these, as I have explained in detail in my book *A*

Survey of Buddhism, correspond to the Five Spiritual Faculties. What Conze terms the Buddhism of Faith and Devotion, with its highly emotional worship of the Buddhas, both historic and 'legendary', and of Bodhisattvas such as Avalokiteshvara, Manjushri and Tara, represents a specialization, as it were, in the Faculty of Faith. The Madhyamika School, or School of the Mean, with its rigorously dialectical approach to Reality, represents a specialization in the Faculty of Wisdom. Similarly the Tantra, which in its esoteric form integrates not only the mind but the physical energies of breath and semen, concentrates on the Faculty of Vigour. The fourth spiritual faculty, that of Concentration, is represented on the theoretical side by the Yogachara and on the practical side by the school which is known, in its Japanese form, as Zen. the Faculty of Mindfulness is represented by the spirit of tolerance which is diffused through all the schools and which holds them together as 'moments' in the Mahayana-concept.

This correspondence between the schools of the Mahayana and the Five Spiritual Faculties gives us an important clue to the nature of Zen. Quite simply, it is that aspect of Mahayana Buddhism which emphasizes the importance of meditation, and specializes therein. This is indicated by the very name of the school. The Chinese term Ch'an-na is a corruption of the Sanskrit Dhyana, the general Indian word for meditative practice and experience, while Zen-na, Zen for short, is the Japanese corruption of the Chinese corruption. Thus the Zen School is really the Dhyana or Meditation School.

At the same time, Zen has its own distinctive features. This becomes obvious as we go a little deeper into the meaning of the word meditation. According to the remarkable man previously mentioned, there are four kinds of Ch'an or Zen. So far as I know, this extremely important traditional classification, which sheds much light on the nature of Zen, has never appeared in English before, and it is unknown to Western Buddhists. I therefore hope that it will be of interest to you.

1. *Tathagata Ch'an* or the classical methods of concentration such as counting the breaths and cultivating a spirit of universal love which were taught by Gautama the Buddha and are common to practically all forms of Buddhism, including Zen. In Zen monasteries the beginner is taught these methods and often practises nothing else for several years.

2. *Patriarchal Ch'an,* i.e. the Ch'an of Hui Neng, the sixth Chinese patriarch of the Zen School. This refers to *The Platform Scripture's* teaching of the identity, or at any rate the inseparability, of Samadhi and Prajna. Hui Neng says, 'Learned Audience, in my system Samadhi and Prajna are fundamental. But do not be under the wrong impression that these two are independent of each other, for they are inseparably united and are not two entities. Samadhi is the quintessence of Prajna, while Prajna is the activity of Samadhi. At the very moment that we attain Prajna, Samadhi is therewith; and vice versa . . . . A disciple should not think that there is a distinction between "Samadhi begets Prajna" and "Prajna begets Samadhi". *(Sutra of Wei Lang,* p. 46). Further, 'Samadhi and Prajna . . . are analogous to a lamp and its light. With the lamp, there is light. Without it, it would be dark. The lamp is the quintessence of the light and the light is the expression of the lamp. In name they are two things, but in substance they are one and the same. It is the same case with Samadhi and Prajna'. *(Sutra of Wei Lang,* p. 47.) Prajna of course means Wisdom in the sense of Transcendental Wisdom. But what does

Samadhi mean? Here there is a great deal of confusion to be cleared up. As one of the Five Spiritual Faculties, Samadhi means simply one-pointedness of mind or concentration. This is the meaning of the term in what we may call general Buddhism, the type of Buddhism codified in, and nowadays represented by the Theravada, and it is in the same sense that Samadhi is to be understood when it is enumerated as the second of the three great stages of progress into which the spiritual path is divided, the first stage being Shila or Morality and the third Prajna or Wisdom. In the Mahayana sutras which form the background of Hui Neng's teaching, however, Samadhi has a quite different meaning. Confusion has been created in the minds of Western students of Zen because they wrongly assumed that the Samadhi which Hui Neng was equating with Prajna was Samadhi in the sense of mental concentration, thus making nonsense of the entire scheme of Buddhist spiritual self-development. In the Mahayana sutras, Samadhi corresponds to the *chetovimutti* or state of conscious spiritual emancipation of the Theravada texts rather than to Samadhi in the sense of concentration. Mahayana Samadhi may well be said to be Enlightenment in its subjective aspect of personal realization. Prajna or Wisdom is the objective aspect of actual manifestation and function in the world, the two of course being inseparable. This Prajna is not the ordinary Prajna of the general Buddhist teaching, consisting of insight into the unsatisfactory, impermanent and unsouled nature of conditioned things, but Maha Prajna, or Great Wisdom, realization of the Voidness – not emptiness but absolute unconditioned reality – of all the phenomena of existence. Collating the general Buddhist teaching with that of the Mahayana sutras we may say that, according to Hui Neng, the entire system of Buddhist spiritual training may be expressed in the formula Shila (Morality)→ Samadhi (Concentration) → Prajna → SAMADHI - PRAJNA = BUDDHAHOOD. While Tathagata Ch'an is concerned with the practice of Concentration, the second term in the series, Patriarchal Ch'an, is concerned with the realization of SAMADHI-PRAJNA, the fourth.

3. *Offspring Ch'an.* This is Ch'an as taught by the spiritual descendants of Hui Neng, especially by the great masters of the fourth, fifth, sixth and seventh generations, who became the founders of the Five Ch'an 'Sects' of China. Whereas Tathagata Ch'an and Patriarchal Ch'an are Indian in form, Offspring Ch'an is characteristically Chinese. Instead of quoting the scriptures and discoursing at length on the philosophy and practice of Zen in the traditional manner, as even Hui Neng does, this kind of Ch'an tries to bring about the experience of Enlightenment in a more direct and concrete manner with the help of seemingly eccentric and bizarre words, sentences and actions. These are the celebrated kung-ans (Japanese koans: literally 'public documents'), or 'concurrent causes' of Enlightenment, such as a sudden shout, a roar of laughter, a gesture, a blow with a staff.

4. *Mouth Ch'an.* This is the Ch'an of people who merely talk about Zen, or write books and articles about it, and never do any practice. When my friend in Kalimpong told me about this kind of Ch'an I remarked that it was very common in the West, where it was the dominant school, with many distinguished masters, and almost a patriarchal succession of its own. He replied, rather sadly, that it was common enough in China too, even in the old

days. On another occasion, when I showed him an article on Zen in a Western Buddhist magazine, he burst into roars of laughter after reading a few sentences. But soon the laughter changed to tears, and he wept bitterly, out of compassion for sincere seekers after truth who were being deceived and misled by the exponents of Mouth Ch'an.

In the course of the next four weeks I shall try to do justice to what Zen has in common with other schools of Buddhism as well as to its own distinctive features. The subject will be dealt with by way of a consideration of a popular traditional verse widely regarded as embodying the essence of Zen. By this means, it is hoped, misunderstanding will be avoided. Before telling you what this verse is, let me briefly touch upon what are, so it seems to me, the three causes for much of the current Western misunderstanding of Zen.

The first cause is our purely intellectual approach. Most Western students derive their knowledge of Zen from books, usually from those of Suzuki. In the beginning this is, of course, unavoidable. Fortunately, at present a number of books on Zen are available which are probably as reliable as books of Zen can be. Such, for example, are the three volumes of Charles Luk's *Ch'an and Zen Teaching* and Trevor Leggett's *First Zen Reader* and *The Tiger's Cave*. Thoughtfully – one might even say contemplatively – read, works of this nature, besides conveying something of the spirit of Zen, make the sensitive reader aware of the limitations of the intellectual approach. As though with one voice they urge him to practise Zen. Unfortunately, only too many people seem to have a perfect intellectual understanding of the fact that Zen cannot be intellectually understood. So thoroughly do they understand the need for practice that the idea of actually practising Zen themselves never occurs to them. Instead, on the basis of their reading and their intellectual knowledge of Zen, they set to work and produce yet another book on the subject. In these books they usually argue at great lengths, as if to convince the unconverted, that books cannot tell you anything about Zen, that the intellect is a hindrance, and that one should cultivate one's intuition. After several hundred pages of discussion, Zen is usually defined, very much to their own satisfaction, as 'the indefinable'. If questioned about meditation, Zen intellectuals of this type are liable to snap back, "I do my meditation while I'm waiting for the traffic lights to change".

Secondly, we try to understand Zen apart from Buddhism. This is like trying to understand the acorn apart from the oak, and is absolutely futile. Zen is an integral part of the total Buddhist tradition. As we have already seen, it is that aspect of the Mahayana which specializes in the practice of meditation. The terminology and techniques of Zen, as well as its doctrines, its scriptures, its spiritual ideal, and its monastic organisation and ordination-lineage, have all been taken over from Buddhism, and even after being given the special development, the characteristic emphasis, that makes them Zen, cannot be understood independently. If we are in personal contact with an enlightened Zen master and are prepared to follow his instructions implicitly, we need not bother about Buddhism. We need not bother even about Zen. But so long as we do not have this advantage we have no alternative but to study Zen as part of Buddhism. Any other course would be as futile as trying to understand the origins and nature of Methodism without reference either to the Church of England or to Christianity.

The last of the three main causes for our misunderstanding of Zen is that we mistake the finger for the moon. According to the Buddhist saying, when one asks, "Where is the moon?" and somebody points it out with his finger saying, "There it is!" one does not stand with eyes rivetted on the finger. One looks from the finger to the moon. In the same way all the teachings and methods of Zen are so many pointers to the experience of Enlightenment. The disciple does not take them for ends in themselves. He utilizes them as helps to the attainment of liberation. Some Western students of Zen, however, fascinated by the apparently bizarre sayings and doings of the later Zen masters, think that *this is Zen.* For instance, they read that when disciple so-and-so questioned Master such-and-such about Zen, the latter, instead of answering, gave him thirty blows with his staff. Giving thirty blows, they think, is Zen. Whenever anybody mentions Zen, therefore, they explain triumphantly, "Aha, thirty blows for you!" and think that they have thereby demonstrated their superior understanding of Zen. Others think that the Tea Ceremony is Zen, or Judo, or Kendo, or Karate. They fail to realize that these are not Zen itself but only expressions of Zen within a certain Far Eastern cultural context. Some even think that Zen is Japanese. If one wanted to be paradoxical, not to say provocative, one could go so far as to say that Zen had nothing whatever to do with Japan.

In the coming weeks, we shall try to avoid misunderstandings of Zen such as those I have described. Now for our verse. It is said to have originated during the Tang Dynasty in China, but nobody knows who composed it. The verse reads:

'A special transmission outside the Scriptures;
No dependence upon words and letters;

Direct pointing to the mind (of man);
Seeing into one's own nature and realizing
Buddhahood'.

Each of the four lines of the verse represents a fundamental principle of the Zen School. Each week, therefore, we shall take up one line for study. In this way, I hope, we shall acquire some insight into the essence of Zen, thus approaching nearer to Enlightenment and broadening and enriching our understanding of the whole Buddhist tradition.

Second Talk

A special transmission outside the Scriptures;

At first sight the idea of a special transmission outside the Scriptures seems quite simple and easy to understand. Had we encountered it in a book we probably would not have given it a second thought, assuming as a matter of course that we understood what was meant. But is this line, the first line of our verse, really so simple as it appears? *'A special transmission outside the Scriptures'*. . . . If we give ourselves time to think, a number of questions suggest themselves.

What are the Scriptures?

What is meant by a 'transmission', or a 'special transmission'?

What is meant by 'outside'? . . .

Let us examine each of these in turn.

First of all the *Scriptures.* All the religions of the world possess sacred books. Christians, for example, have the Bible; Muslims the Qu'ran; and Hindus the Vedas. Similarly Buddhists have what is known as the Tri-pitaka. *Tri* means 'three', while *Pitaka* means 'basket' or, by extension of meaning, 'collection'. The Tri-pitaka is therefore the 'Three Basketfuls' or 'Three Collections' of Buddhist sacred texts. According to some authorities, in the early days of Buddhism the bundles of palm-leaf manuscript on which the texts were inscribed were divided, according to subject matter, into three groups that were kept, for convenience of reference, in three wicker containers. Some, however, suggest that the term refers to the way in which earth and other excavated material was passed from hand to hand in baskets down a line of workmen. In the same way the monks handed down the sacred traditions, first in oral and then in literary form, from generation to generation. The 'Three Basketfuls' or 'Three Collections' are:

1. The Vinaya Pitaka or Collection of Monastic Discipline. In its present form this consists mainly of the rules governing the Monastic Order, including the circumstances in which these were promulgated, interspersed with a great deal of biographical, historical and doctrinal matter. The original nucleus of this Pitaka seems to have been a short life of the Buddha.

2. The Sutra Pitaka or Collection of Discourses, Dialogues and Sayings of the Buddha on various moral and spiritual topics. This is the most important collection.

3. The Abhidharma Pitaka or Collection of Higher Doctrine. This is a systematic arrangement and scholastic analysis of material found in the Sutra Pitaka.

Traditionally the entire contents of the Tripitaka are regarded as Buddha-vachana or Word of the Buddha. The Buddha Himself, of course, wrote nothing. Like Socrates and Christ, He taught orally. Those who remembered what He had said told His sayings to their disciples; they told theirs, and in this way the Teaching was transmitted to posterity. Only after five hundred years, approximately, of oral transmission was the Teaching committed to writing. Much, no doubt, had been added. Much, perhaps, had been lost. At present there are extant in the Buddhist world three major editions of the Tripitaka.

1. The Chinese San Tsang or 'Three Treasuries' (i.e. Tri-pitaka) in 55 volumes.

2. The Tibetan Kanjur (='Buddha-vachana') in 100 or 108 volumes.

Both these editions consist mainly of translations from the Sanskrit, many of the original texts having since been lost.

3. The Pali Tipitaka in 45 volumes (Royal Thai edition).

This is the only version of the canon to have survived complete in the language in which it was originally compiled.

The three editions of the Tripitaka possess a great deal of material in common. The biggest difference is that while the Chinese and Tibetan editions include the Mahayana sutras the Pali edition omits them.

Even when allowance is made for overlapping, the Buddhist Scriptures are far more voluminous than those of any other religion. The Bible consists of 64 books; but the Chinese San Tsang, for example, contains 1,662 independent works, several of them almost as long as the entire Bible. Though much of this vast literature has been translated into English and other European languages, an even greater part of it remains untranslated. Thanks to the labours of the Pali Text Society, the Pali Tipitaka has been translated almost in its entirety. A number of the most important Mahayana sutras are also available. Kern has translated the *Saddharma-pundarika,* Izumi the *Vimalakirti-nirdesa,* Suzuki the *Lankavatara,* Lamotte the *Sandhinirmochana* (in French), Luk the *Surangama-samadhi.* Above all, in the greatest individual achievement in this field in modern times, Conze has translated the whole *Prajnaparamita* or 'Perfection of Wisdom' group of sutras, consisting of more than thirty independent works.

A great deal of basic material is thus available for study. Unfortunately, the majority of English Buddhists and students of Buddhism fail to take advantage of the fact. Very few study regularly and systematically even a tithe of what has been translated. Consequently their knowledge of Buddhism remains vague and superficial. Some, indeed, appear to read anything rather than the Scriptures.

Classics of Christian mysticism, books about Pak Subud, even the romances of Lobsang Rampa, are eagerly devoured, while essential texts like the *Diamond Sutra* and the *Sutta-nipata* remain unread. This is not to say that there is anything wrong in reading the classics of Christian mysticism and deriving inspiration from them. But if one considers oneself a Buddhist and claims to be seriously following the Path of the Buddha, it is strange that one should not make every effort to acquaint oneself with the basic literature of the subject. No doubt the Buddhist Scriptures, even in the best translation, are often unattractive in form and obscure and difficult in content. But if we want to participate in the spiritual riches of Buddhism the effort to understand them must be made. After all, if we want to take up engineering, or medicine, or even pig-breeding, we have to put in a certain amount of intellectual hard work, we have to study. Buddhism demands no less. Ask yourselves, therefore, those of you who consider yourselves Buddhists, when it was that you last read a translation of one of the Buddhist sacred books. The answer might surprise you.

Some, of course, try to rationalize the situation and justify themselves. Western advocates of Zen, for instance, are fond of citing the example of Hui Neng, the Sixth Chinese Patriarch, whom Far Eastern Buddhist art sometimes depicts in the act of tearing up *The Diamond Sutra*. They forget that if he did in fact do any such thing (there is no mention of the incident in *The Platform Scripture)* it was only after realizing the import of the Sutra and that, in any case, he probably knew the entire text by heart. In Zen monasteries scriptures like *The Diamond Sutra The Heart Sutra* and *The Kwannon Sutra* are not only studied but learned by heart and liturgically recited as an aid to the spiritual life. It is interesting to observe that those who neglect, and even depreciate, the primary sources, can be fanatical in their devotion to quite secondary ones. The Word of the Buddha resounds unheeded, but Suzuki and a host of lesser lights are hearkened to with eager attention.

Whether our interest is in Buddhism in general or in one or another of its special forms, we cannot by-pass the Scriptures. In them are contained the original records of the transcendental experiences of the Buddha and His enlightened disciples. Without a preliminary intellectual understanding of these records we have no means of knowing what it is that we, as Buddhists, including followers of Zen, are trying to attain and what is the method of its attainment. The only thing that can absolve us from study of the Scriptures is regular personal contact with an enlightened teacher, who is the living embodiment of the Scriptures. Such a teacher is difficult to come by even in the East. In the absence of personal contact of this kind the Scriptures are indispensable.

So much for what is meant by the Scriptures. Now we come to the *transmission* or *special transmission*. What is meant by this? According to the dictionary the literal meaning of the word transmit is 'to send across', also to pass on or hand down. Here we have the idea of Buddhism itself as *something transmitted*, something handed down. On the biological plane, life is transmitted from parents to children. On the spiritual plane, there is a transmission of Buddhism, or the Dharma. This transmission takes place between master and disciple. Hence the importance of this relationship. It is, in fact, the axis upon which the whole world of Buddhism turns. There are a number of different types of transmission of Buddhism, or rather, the transmission can take place on different levels. Four principal transmissions are enumerated.

1. *Transmission of Ordination.* Broadly speaking ordination is of three kinds: as a lay brother or lay sister *(upasaka, upasika),* as a monk or nun *(bhikshu, bhikshuni),* and as a Bodhisattva. These three categories of ordained persons make up the Sangha or Spiritual Community in the socio-ecclesiastical sense of the term. Each ordination involves the adoption of a certain spiritual attitude and the observance of a certain rule. The lay brother or lay sister, who can be ordained by any monk, nun or Bodhisattva, goes for refuge to the Buddha, Dharma and Sangha and undertakes to observe the Ten Precepts, that is to say, to abstain from harming living beings, from taking what is not given, from sexual misconduct, from false, harsh, frivolous and backbiting speech, as well as from greed, hatred and wrong views. A monk must be ordained by a chapter of not less than five other monks including an elder *(sthavira)* or monk of at least ten years, standing in the Order. Nuns require a double ordination, once by a chapter of monks and once by a chapter of nuns. Both monks and nuns renounce the household life, devote all their energies to the realization of Nirvana, and observe a basic rule of 150 clauses. The four most important clauses relate to abstention from sexual intercourse, from theft, from murder and incitement to suicide, and from making false claims to spiritual attainments. A Bodhisattva is ordained ideally by a Buddha, but in practice by any senior Bodhisattva. In special circumstances self-ordination is permitted. He

(or she) develops the Will to Enlightenment for the sake of all sentient beings and observes a rule consisting (according to the Indo-Tibetan tradition) of 18 major and 46 minor provisions, all strongly altruistic in emphasis. The three kinds of ordination are not mutually exclusive. A lay brother or lay sister, or monk or nun, may in addition be ordained as a Bodhisattva. In the Mahayana Buddhist world Bodhisattva ordination tends to supersede all other kinds of ordination..

2. *Transmission of the Scriptures.* As we have seen, the Buddha Himself wrote nothing. After centuries of oral transmission, His words were committed to writing and preserved in the form of palm-leaf manuscripts. Eventually the manuscripts were printed in book form. These books, in the three editions described, constitute the Buddhist Scriptures. Traditionally, one of the principal functions of the monks was to preserve incorrupt the pure and authentic Word of the Buddha, first in oral and subsequently in literary form. They alone had time for the prodigious feat of memorization involved. Once the 'Scriptures' had been committed to writing, though, the importance of the monks as preservers and transmitters diminished. But they continued to be the custodians of the correct interpretation of the texts. This interpretation was often embodied in commentaries, which gave not the author's personal understanding of the texts so much as the traditional interpretation which he had received from his teachers along with the texts themselves. In some parts of the Buddhist world one is still not considered to have mastered the Scriptures unless one has studied them with a teacher. Reading the printed page by oneself is not sufficient. One has to learn, at the same time, the correct interpretation,

which can be done only with the help of a teacher 'in the succession'. Tibetan Buddhism still retains the institution of *lun* or 'authorization'. Students are permitted to read or recite a sacred text only after it has been read aloud in their ear, with explanations, by their teacher. Some texts, of course, require more explanation than others. But in all cases the principle of a proper *transmission* of the Scripture *and* their meaning is upheld.

3. *Transmission of the Doctrine.* By 'Doctrine' is meant, in this context, the systematic presentation of the Teaching, as contained in the Scriptures, in terms of a logically coherent intellectual structure. The expression may be considered roughly equivalent to the terms 'Buddhist thought' and 'Buddhist philosophy'. Such presentations seem to have originated with the 'lists of lists' which were compiled after the Buddha's death, perhaps even during His lifetime. These were more or less complete enumerations of the various sets of related doctrinal topics – the Five Aggregates, the Nine Holy Persons, the Twelve Links, and so on – in which, for mnemonic purposes, the Teaching had been cast. As presentations of the Teaching the 'lists of lists' were systematic only in the purely formal sense. More truly systematic are the *shastras,* such as the Abhidharma treatises, the Five Books of Maitreya, and *The Awakening of Faith in the Mahayana.* In India there were four different, practically simultaneous, transmissions of the Doctrine, in the form of the four 'philosophical' schools of the Vaibhashikas, the Sautrantikas, the Vijnanavadins and the Madhyamikas. These were systematic presentations of the Teaching in terms, respectively, of naive realism, critical realism, idealism and absolutism. All four transmissions continued,

with amplifications and extentions, in Tibet and the Far East. In China the Transmission of the Doctrine was safeguarded by the great indigenous schools of the Hua-yen (=Avatamsaka or 'Flower-Ornament') and T'ien-t'ai, characterized respectively by Takakusu as the totalistic and phenomenological (Mahayanistic) schools.

4. *Transmission of the Spirit of Buddhism,* This is the most important transmission of all. It is to this type of transmission that the verse refers when it speaks of a special transmission outside the Scriptures. Though only the Scriptures are actually mentioned, the transmission is to be understood as taking place outside ordination and outside doctrine as well.

How did this transmission of the spirit of Buddhism begin? According to tradition, the Buddha was once seated in the midst of a great concourse of His disciples. Hundreds of Bodhisattvas and Arahants, monks and nuns, lay brothers and lay sisters, were present, as well as various orders of celestial beings. All were silent, waiting for the Buddha to speak. This is, of course, the customary setting for a discourse by the Buddha. But on this occasion, instead of speaking, the Master simply held up amidst the silence of the assembly a golden flower.... Only Mahakashyapa, one of the oldest disciples, famed for his austerity, understood the meaning of the Buddha's action, and smiled. The Buddha then said: 'I am the owner of the Eye of the wonderful Dharma, which is Nirvana, the Mind, the mystery of reality and non-reality, and the gate of the transcendental truth. I now hand it over to Mahakashyapa'. This was the transmission.

What happened? It is very difficult to explain. When the Buddha held up the golden flower (not when he spoke, which was only for the benefit of the other disciples, who had failed to understand the significance of his action) there took place a direct communication of truth from one mind to another, from a supremely enlightened mind to one that was almost so, and needing only the most delicate of touches to bring it to perfection. The transmission from the Buddha was analogous to what happens, at an infinitely lower level of experience, between two people who understand each other very well. A sign or a look, the significance of which is a mystery to everyone else, suffices to convey a whole world of meaning. So it is on the highest spiritual plane.

Mahakashyapa transmitted the spirit of the Dharma to Ananda, who had been the Buddha's personal attendant during the last twenty years of His earthly life, he to his disciple Sanakavasa, and so on. From Mahakashyapa in the 5th century B.C. to Bodhidharma in the 6th century A.D. it continued to be transmitted down a long line of spiritual masters, some otherwise unknown to fame, others among the most distinguished names in Indian Buddhism. The list of these masters, who are traditionally regarded as the Twenty-seven (including Bodhidharma, Twenty-eight) Indian 'Patriarchs' of the Zen school, is as follows:

(1) Mahakashyapa
(2) Ananda
(3) Sanakavasa
(4) Upagupta (spiritual teach of the Emperor Ashoka)
(5) Dhritaka
(6) Michchaka
(7) Vasumitra (the earliest historian of Buddhism)
(8) Buddhanandi

(9) Buddhamitra
(10) Parshva (? President of Fourth Council, the Council of Kanishka)
(11) Punyayashas
(12) Ashvaghosha (author of *Life of the Buddha*, *Awakening of Faith in the Mahayana*, etc.)
(13) Kapimala
(14) Nagarjuna (rediscoverer of the 'Perfection of Wisdom' sutras and founder of the Madhyamika School)
(15) Kanadeva (= Aryadeva, co-founder of the Madhyamika School)
(16) Rahulata
(17) Sanghanandi
(18) Gayasata
(19) Kumarata
(20) Jayata
(21) Vasubandhu (author of *Abhidharma-kosha*, etc., and founder of Vijnanavada School)
(22) Monorhita
(23) Haklena
(24) Aryasimha
(25) Basiasita
(26) Punyamitra
(27) Prajnatara
(28) Bodhidharma

A study of this list reveals the close connection between Zen and what may be termed the central tradition of Indian Buddhism.

It was the celebrated Bodhidharma, the twenty-eighth Indian Patriarch – whom tradition depicts crossing the ocean on a reed – who 'took' Zen to China, thus becoming the First Chinese Patriarch of the School. What he took to China, of course, was not the Zen School as we know it today, complete with doctrines, scriptures and temple organization, but the living spirit of Buddhism. This spirit he transmitted to his disciple Hui K'o, he to his disciple, and so on down a succession of altogether six spiritual masters. These masters are known as the Six Chinese Patriarchs of the Zen School, as follows:

(1) Bodhidharma
(2) Hui K'o
(3) Seng Ts'an
(4) Tao Hsin
(5) Hung Jen
(6) Hui Neng (Wei Lang)

Such was the spiritual genius of Hui Neng, the sixth and last Chinese Patriarch, that he was able to transmit the spirit of Buddhism not to one disciple only, as the custom apparently had been hitherto, but to forty-three. Thereafter there were many different lines of transmission, no one of which could be regarded as the main one. Five lines were however of special importance, of which two continue down to the present day. These two lines are represented by the Soto and Rinzai Schools of contemporary Japanese Buddhism.

Zen is essentially concerned with the fourth type of transmission, the transmission of the living spirit of Buddhism. This transmission is made possible through the high level of spiritual communication existing between master and disciple, usually within a context of meditation and study. Ordination and observance of the monastic discipline, scriptural studies, and doctrinal knowledge, are all important, but only as means to an end, never as ends in themselves. The real thing, the only thing that ultimately matters, is the spiritual – better transcendental – experience, the experience of Enlightenment. If this is not transmitted the transmission of all the rest is a waste of time. At best it is a cultural curiosity. Amending our previous definition, which was provisional, we may now say of Zen not merely that it is that aspect of the Mahayana which specializes in meditation, but that it represents a transmission of the living spirit of Buddhism with the help of the three main kinds of Ch'an described in the previous talk.

Thirdly and lastly, what is meant by *outside* the Scriptures? The Scriptures consist of words. Words convey ideas. In the case of the Scriptures these ideas point in the direction of a spiritual experience. Zen, we have seen, is concerned primarily with this experience. It is not concerned with ordination, Scriptures, or doctrine; or rather, it is concerned with them only as means to the experience of Enlightenment, not as ends in themselves. But it certainly does not dispense with them altogether, on principle as it were. Instead, it follows a middle path. Distinguished from the Scriptures but not divided from them, its own distinctive transmission makes use of the Scriptures without becoming attached to them and without being enslaved by them. This is what is meant by 'outside'.

We have now answered the three questions which suggested themselves at the beginning of this talk and have understood, I hope, the sense in which Zen is said to be 'A special transmission outside the Scriptures'.

Third Talk

No dependence on words or letters;

This week we are faced by a difficulty. 'No dependence upon words and letters', declares the second line of our verse, continuing its definition of Zen. This means I shall have to talk about not depending upon words and letters, but in so doing I shall in fact be dependent upon words and letters, or at least upon words and sounds. This is self-contradictory. Ideally I ought to expound the line by sitting in absolute silence for an hour. And an excellent exposition it would be! But if I did this you would probably all become restless and dissatisfied, and wouldn't put anything in the collection plate when you left, or at any rate not so much as usual. People value words; they do not value silence. So I suppose I shall have to try and do my best with words.

'No dependence upon words and letters'. The line suggests that usually there is such a dependence. Let us examine the matter a little, first with regard to our dependence on words and letters in a general sense, and then with regard to our dependence on them where spiritual things are concerned.

Take the case of what we call our knowledge. We say we know this or know that. But what do we really mean? We mean, surely, that we have read it somewhere, or heard about it, or seen it on television. We have no *direct* knowledge whatever. It is all based on hearsay, on second-hand, third-hand and tenth-hand information, on conjecture and gossip. We consider, for instance, that we know what is going on in the world at large, what is happening in distant places – India, Rhodesia, Indonesia, etc. But whence is our 'knowledge' derived? From words and letters.

From the radio and the newspapers, from snatches of conversation overheard in the Tube, from chance remarks at parties. How great is our dependence! The thought is quite a horrifying one. Supposing there were no radios, no newspapers, we would 'know' very little of what went on in the world. We would have fewer thoughts, fewer ideas. Being less cluttered up mentally, we would be better able to concentrate on things near at hand. We would be able to live more intensely. Perhaps we would be closer to reality.

This was, of course, the condition of our ancestors in bygone days, even as it is still the condition of many people in the 'undeveloped' countries. Compared with us, our ancestors knew very little of what was going on in the great world that lay outside the gates of their own village or township. Vague rumours reached them from the distant capital, and usually that was all. Sometimes, of course, they saw armies marching past, and sometimes armies devastated with fire and sword, but despite beating drums and flying colours, ordinary folk often did not understand what the war was about or who was fighting whom. Occasionally men were conscripted. Otherwise, apart from natural calamities, the stream of life flowed on placid and undisturbed from year to year and from generation to generation. I am not trying to idealize the past. I am only trying to point out how much our knowledge depends upon words and letters and how little on direct personal experience, and that this dependence is moreover, both proportionally and absolutely, greater now than ever before in history.

This is true in all fields. Take any subject that we think we 'know'. Take botany, or the history of art, or any other branch of human knowledge, from astronomy to zoology. By far the greater part of our knowledge of these subjects, if not the whole of it, is second-hand. Hardly any of it is original, the result of our own independent thought and discovery. Inheriting as it were a great stockpile of knowledge from the past, we go through life, for the most part, without adding to it so much as a single grain of our own. Originality would seem to be the prerogative of genius.

In everyday life all this, though perhaps regrettable, does not matter very much. We manage to get along somehow. From the Zen point of view, however, it is nevertheless important to realize what is actually happening. It might be interesting to perform an experiment. As you sit here, fold your hands and close your eyes, just as you do for meditation. Forget all you have ever learned from books, newspapers, magazines, radio, television and the advertisements. Forget even talks, lectures and discussions. How much knowledge would you then have left? Very little indeed. If we were to perform the experiment regularly the experience would be a very salutary one. We should then realize how little we really know. To know that we do not know is the beginning of wisdom.

From our general dependence on words and letters let us now turn to our dependence on them where spiritual things are concerned. We have, let us assume, a certain amount of religious knowledge. We know about Buddhism. We know about the Four Noble Truths and the Noble Eightfold Path; about karma and rebirth, Nirvana, and Dependent Origination; about Shunyata, Bodhisattvas, and the Pure Land. What a lot we know! We even know about Zen. Now where has all this knowledge come from? From books and lectures. Ultimately, of course, it comes from the Scriptures, a survey of which I attempted to give last week. Now the Scriptures consist of words and letters. On words and letters, therefore, is our knowledge of Buddhism dependent. Hence it is all second-hand, not based on direct, personal experience and perception.

Let us perform another experiment. Let us put aside all knowledge of Buddhism that depends on words and letters, all that we have not experienced and verified for ourselves. Probably we shall have to discard quite a lot. Do we really *know* what Nirvana is? What about Shunyata? Put them aside too if necessary. At the end of the experiment how much real knowledge is left? Perhaps none at all.

We should not think we have lost anything, however. In fact there is a great gain. As we saw last week, Zen is concerned with the experience of the living spirit of Buddhism, and with the transmission of that spirit. For Zen nothing else matters. Nothing must be allowed to stand in the way. This is what makes Zen so 'ruthless'. Zen has no hesitation about burning holy Buddha-images or tearing up the sacred books if these come in the way. But what is it that comes in the way more than anything else? What is it that most of all prevents us from having a real knowledge of Buddhism, based on our own experience? Can anybody tell me? . . . . You are all silent. Surely the greatest obstacle is *to think that we know.* Until this obstacle has been removed, no progress is possible. Here, more than anywhere else, is the beginning of wisdom. It is also the beginning of Enlightenment, the beginning of progress: *to know that we do not know.*

Such knowledge involves distinguishing between what we know at second hand, from the Scriptures, and what we know from experience. This is what Zen means when it urges us not to confuse the two kinds of knowledge. If we do confuse them no spiritual progress is possible. Unfortunately we are guilty of this confusion all the time. It is, in fact, part of our general psychological conditioning. Having failed to distinguish thoughts from things, we then fail to distinguish words from thoughts. We think that if we can label a thing we have understood it. Take, for example, Nirvana. This is essentially a spiritual principle, or transcendental reality, and can be thought of in various ways. For instance, it can be thought of in terms of the complete cessation of craving. Since we understand what is meant by the words 'cessation of craving' we think that we know what Nirvana is! When, therefore, in some non-Buddhist work, we come across the idea of freedom from craving, we at once triumphantly exclaim "Ah yes, Nirvana!" At once we slap on the label. We think we 'know' that the state of freedom from craving mentioned in the non-Buddhist work and the Buddhist Nirvana are one and the same. All that we have in fact done is to equate thoughts and words. We are not dealing directly with things, with realities, at all. At best we are dealing with thoughts about things, or often with just words.

Conceptualizing and verbalizing activity of this sort is only too common in the West. People talk far too much. They always want to affix ready-made labels to their experiences. It is as though they were unable to enjoy the beauty of a flower until they had given it its correct botanical classification and a Latin name. We have to learn the value of silence, not only physical silence, but the silence of thoughts, the silence of the mind. In this connection I remember an anecdote told me, many years ago, by an Indian friend of mine, an elder brother in the Order. Some years previously this friend had paid a visit to Germany, where he gave some lectures on Buddhism.

One morning a German Buddhist lady came to see him. As he was in the midst of writing a letter, and wanted to catch the post, he asked her to wait in an adjoining room. He had only been writing for a few minutes, however, when the door suddenly burst open, and the German lady violently exclaimed, "I shall go mad if I stay here much longer. *There's no one to talk to!*". As he came to the end of the story my friend threw up his hands in mock despair, as if to say, "What hope is there of spreading Buddhism among such people?"

Some things there are which can be experienced and also thought about and described in words. Others, though capable of being experienced, transcend thought and speech. At best they can only be indicated, or suggested, or hinted at. Such are the realities, or aspects of reality, of which we speak in such terms as 'Enlightenment', 'Nirvana', 'Buddhahood'. All these terms are used only provisionally. They give us a certain amount of practical guidance, some idea of the quarter in which to look, the direction towards which we have to orient our spiritual strivings, but their validity is only relative. They do not really define the goal. In using them we say, therefore, in the absolute sense, nothing at all. Hence in the *Lankavatara Sutra* the Buddha declares that from the night of His Supreme Enlightenment to the night of His Final Passing Away He has not uttered a single word. Between the two events lay forty-five years of untiring earthly ministry. During that period He had taught thousands, perhaps hundreds of thousands, of people. Hardly a day had gone by without discourses, dialogues, answers to questions. Yet in reality nothing had been said because nothing can be said about reality. All His words had been pointers to what is beyond words. As

Ashvaghosha says, "We use words to get free from words until we reach the pure wordless Essence".

Even better known and more striking is Vimalakirti's 'thunderlike silence'. Vimalakirti, the great householder Bodhisattva of Vaishali, was sick, and the Buddha asked Shariputra to go and enquire after his health. The great disciple declines, however, as he had once been admonished by Vimalakirti and feels unworthy of the mission. All the other disciples, including the Bodhisattvas, also protest their unworthiness, and for the same reason; all have been severely discomfited by Vimalakirti at some time or another. Eventually Manjushri, the great Bodhisattva of Wisdom, agrees to comply with the Buddha's request, and goes to see Vimalakirti with a vast retinue. There is a great deal of discussion, and much subtle dialectic. Eventually the nature of the Not-Two Doctrine comes up for discussion. Various interpretations are given by those present. One says, "Purity and impurity make two. If you see the real nature of impurity, then there is no state of purity, and you conform to the state of purity. This is entering the gate of the Not-Two Doctrine". Another says, "Samsara and Nirvana make two. See the (true) nature of Samsara, and then there is no Samsara, no bondage, no liberation, no burning and no cessation". Finally Manjushri is asked for his opinion and replies, "According to my idea, to have no word and no speech, no showing and no awareness about any of the dharmas, and to keep away from all questions and answers, is to enter the gate of the Not-Two Doctrine". His interpretation is greatly applauded. Manjushri then asks Vimalakirtri to speak. But "Vimalakirtri kept silent, without a word". This is the 'thunderlike silence' of Vimalakirti.

So long as we are dependent on words and letters,

allowing ourselves to become enslaved by them instead of making use of them, we shall be unable to realize that which transcends words and letters. We shall, at the same time, confuse the two kinds of knowledge, thinking that we know something when we have merely heard it or read about it. For this reason Zen insists that there must be 'No dependence on words and letters'. Not that words are entirely useless. As I have said at the beginning of the talk, in communicating the truth of no dependence on words and letters one is inevitably dependent on words and letters. Thus we find ourselves back where we started from.

At this point an important question arises. If in Zen there is no dependence on words and letters, then on what *are* we to depend? This question will be dealt with next week, when we consider the third line of our verse.

Fourth Talk

Direct pointing to the mind (of man);

Today we are dealing with the third line of our verse, 'Direct pointing to the mind (of man)', and hoping to find there an answer to the question with which we concluded last week's talk – the question of what, according to Zen, we are to depend on, if there is to be no dependence on words and letters. Like the two previous lines of the verse, the line with which we are now concerned appears, at first sight, to consist of a quite simple and straightforward statement, something that everybody can understand. But this is not so. Before its meaning can become clear to us there is, in fact, a certain amount of obscurity to be resolved. This obscurity is not due to any vagueness on the part of the unknown composer of the verse, much less still on the part of Zen itself, but is simply the result of a characteristically Chinese attempt to pack the maximum amount of meaning into the minimum number of words. The meaning of the verse can be clarified by a consideration of three questions, all of which are interconnected.

What is meant by 'mind'?

Why does Zen insist on pointing to the mind rather than to anything else?

What is the significance of *direct* pointing?

First of all, the meaning of the word mind. In the original Chinese, this is *hsin*. When I was in Kalimpong the hermit friend about whom I told you in the first talk once gave me a detailed explanation of the nine principal meanings of the word in Chinese literature, including Buddhist literature. Fortunately, in the present context we do not need to concern ourselves with all of these. Broadly speaking *hsin* corresponds to the Indian (Pali and Sanskrit) word *chitta,* which it usually translates. *Chitta* is mind in the widest and most general sense of the term, emotional and conative, as well as intellectual and rational. Some scholars, however, prefer to render *chitta* or *hsin* by heart', others by 'soul'. Suzuki, for instance, in some of his early works, such as his excellent *Outlines of Mahayana Buddhism* and his invaluable translation of Ashvaghosha's *Awakening of Faith in the Mahayana* regularly translates *chitta* as 'soul'. Both renderings are apt to be misleading. In this context *chitta* or *hsin* is not heart as opposed to brain, in the sense of intellect, but rather the totality of mental life and activity which includes them both. It is more like the *psyche* in the Jungian sense of the term. Similarly *chitta* or *hsin* is not 'soul', because this term has, in English, connotations which are quite foreign to Buddhism. Today we are therefore sticking to 'mind' as the best working equivalent of both the Chinese and the Indian term. In any case, at this stage of our enquiry it is unnecessary for us to pay much attention to subtle differences of psychological terminology, and the general English term 'mind' will serve our purpose quite well.

Having warned us not to depend upon words and letters, that is to say on second-hand knowledge of Reality, Zen tells us, as it were, to depend on the mind. This answers the question with which we were left at the end of last week. Zen declares, in effect, DEPEND ON YOUR OWN MIND. That is to say, depend on yourself, for psychologically speaking the mind is the self. Don't look without, don't allow your attention to be distracted by the multiplicity of external phenomena. Look within. This idea is of course not peculiar to Zen. It runs through the whole of Buddhism. In the *Dhammapada,* for instance the

Buddha declares that self-conquest is the greatest of all victories, that the self is its own refuge, its own master, and that purity and impurity depend upon one's own self. Here attention is clearly directed to the subject of experience rather than to its objective content – to the feeling, knowing, willing mind rather than to the external universe. Similar in spirit are the maxim inscribed in the Temple of Apollo at Delphi, "Know thyself", and the *Tao Teh Ching's* saying, "He who knows others is wise; he who knows himself is enlightened". In pointing to the mind, and suggesting that we depend on that rather than on anything else, Zen gives the well known idea its own special emphasis.

This emphasis is by no means superfluous. Indeed it is necessary at all times. People who have reached a certain level of maturity, or who enjoy a certain amount of leisure, tend to become bored and dissatisfied. They become bored and dissatisfied with their jobs, with their wives and families, with books and theatres, with radio and television, with work and with play, with the society to which they belong and the age into which they have been born, with laughter and with tears, with poetry, music and art, with the face of nature and the form of man. Eventually they become bored and dissatisfied with themselves. In this state of boredom and dissatisfaction, of weariness and disgust, even, they start vaguely searching for something – they know not what. Giving it a name, they call it Truth, Reality. Others speak of it in terms of peace, happiness, ultimate satisfaction. Yet others make use of a specifically religious terminology. They speak in terms of God, salvation, Enlightenment, and so on. They even speak in terms of Zen. But however different the ways in which they speak of that for which they are searching, they all agree in searching for it *outside themselves.* Sometimes, of course, they find what they are looking for and establish a relation of dependence on it. They then think that they have succeeded in their quest, that boredom and dissatisfaction have been dispelled. But in reality they have failed. All that has happened is that they have fallen victim to a projection.

As a psychological phenomenon projection is quite familiar to us. In order to avoid having to recognize, and possibly come to terms with, something in ourselves, we unconsciously attribute it to other people. This repressed and projected factor is usually something that we experience as unpleasant or bad, something of which we are ashamed or afraid. We may be, for example, cold, hard, and selfish, completely lacking in warmth and affection. So we criticize other people for being like this. We complain, sometimes with bitterness, that our friends and relations are unkind and unsympathetic, that they trample upon our feelings, that they do not love us. We may even attribute feelings of coldness and hostility to the universe as a whole. All that we are really doing is projecting onto other people, or onto the outside world, our own personal defects. This sort of psychological projection goes on the whole time. Though extreme cases are rare, an element of projection enters into almost all our negative assessments of other people. If we are watchful we can often catch ourselves out. Just as another experiment, in the course of the coming week try to discover what it is you most dislike in others, what you most often criticize and condemn them for. A little elementary self-analysis may reveal that those very qualities are hidden in the depths of your own mind and that in criticizing others in this way you are, in fact, unconsciously criticizing yourself.

Not only bad qualities but good ones too can be projected. These are not things of which we are ashamed or afraid, but capacities existing at a very deep level which we have so far been unable to develop. Sometimes we may be unaware of the possibility of developing them. We project, for example, the quality of love. Feeling the need for love, but being unable to develop it within ourselves, we try to find it outside and receive it from there. In other words we project. Good though a quality may be in itself, the projecting of it, however, is bad inasmuch as this projection stands in the way of full self-integration. In the case of love we cannot, in fact, truly receive it until we are able to give it, and we cannot give love until it has been developed.

It is possible to go even further than this. Projection is not only psychological but spiritual. All men are capable of developing their vague glimmerings of understanding and their intermittent impulses of kindness into the supreme wisdom and infinite compassion of Perfect Buddhahood. All are capable of gaining Enlightenment. But we do not do this. Instead, we project our own potential Enlightenmen as it were outside ourselves, onto another person, onto the figure of the Buddha for instance, and then proceed to establish a relationship with it, that is to say, to worship the Buddha, or at least to venerate Him as the supremely wise and infinitely compassionate Teacher. This does not mean that the Buddha was not enlightened, or that the Buddha-ideal of our religious imagination is nothing but a projection, even a spiritual projection. It means that in the last resort we have to satisfy our need for Enlightenment by developing it within ourselves rather than by becoming parasitic on the Buddha's Enlightenment. Not that spiritual projection has no place at all in the religious life, or that faith and worship are wrong. Spiritual projection represents a very important, and for most of us long continuing, intermediate stage, and as such it has its legitimate place in the total scheme of spiritual development. But *ultimately* it is a hindrance.

Zen, which adopts the absolute standpoint, therefore points to the mind. It calls for a complete withdrawal of *all* projections, positive and negative, psychological and spiritual. It says, "Depend on the mind, depend on yourself". Within this context Enlightenment could be defined as the complete absence of projection.

So far we have considered Zen's pointing to the mind in a very general way. The time has come to be more specific. Zen points to the mind – but to which mind? Mind exists on many different levels, many different planes; it has various aspects, various functions. For instance there are the perceiving mind, the thinking and considering mind, and Absolute Mind. To which of these does Zen point? In a general way, of course, it points to them all, to mind as distinct from matter, as distinct from the external world. But specifically it points to Absolute Mind. It points to the Mind beyond the mind, to the Buddha-nature within, and tells us to rely upon that.

At this point our first question, 'What is meant by mind?' starts overlapping the second, 'Why does Zen insist on pointing to the mind rather than to anything else?' Mind is the point of contact with Reality. Absolute Mind *is* Reality. In pointing to the mind, therefore, Zen points to Reality, points to Enlightenment, which is the experience of Reality, points to the Buddha-nature. This is why it points to the mind in preference to anything else.

We can now see more clearly the nature of the

connection between Zen and meditation. We can understand why Zen is the *Meditation* School. Contrary to what is sometimes thought, meditation is not just a matter of concentration-exercises successfully performed. Meditation may be defined as the persistent and methodical attempt to see Reality within. Ordinarily our attention is directed outwards, towards the world. When we take up the practice of meditation, however, we learn to withdraw our attention from external objects, to disengage the senses from their respective stimuli, and to centre attention within. This attitude of withdrawal finds expression in the posture normally adopted for meditation, when we sit with legs folded beneath us and hands resting, one above the other, on top of the crossed ankles. The eyes are closed, representing the exclusion not only of visual stimuli, but of all sense-impressions whatsoever. With practice it becomes possible to keep the mind centred within for longer and longer periods. This eventually results in a permanent shifting of the centre of attention from the external world to the mind itself, so that even when we are engaged in external activities a degree of inner recollection and awareness persists.

The next step we have to take is to make the mind progressively purer, clearer, and more luminous. That is to say, having turned from the external world to the mind, we now have to turn from the lower mind to the higher mind. In the general tradition which Zen shares with all other forms of Buddhism, this progress is represented by the four *rupadhyanas*, or states of meditative consciousness associated with the world of form, and the four *arupa-dhyanas,* or states of meditative consciousness associated with the formless world. These are usually regarded as together constituting one continuous series. The first of the four states of meditative consciousness associated with the world of form consists of the five psychic factors of thought, both initial and sustained, rapture, bliss, and one-pointedness. In the second of these states thought is eliminated, and in the third, rapture. In the fourth, bliss is replaced by equanimity. One-pointedness is the only psychic factor which remains constant throughout. Indeed, it grows in intensity as the other factors are eliminated and it absorbs the energy invested in them. The four states of meditative consciousness associated with the formless world are known as the Sphere of Infinite Space, the Sphere of Infinite Consciousness, the Sphere of No-thingness, and the Sphere of Neither Perception nor Non-perception. These names tell us very little about the real nature of these states, which represent still higher and more refined experiences of one-pointedness and unification.

Even when the ascent has been made from the lower to the higher mind, and the eight states of meditative consciousness have all been experienced in their fullness, the limits of meditation have not been reached. The eight states are relative or mundane in character. They are not absolute, not transcendental. Reality has not yet been seen. Having turned from the lower to the higher mind we must finally turn, therefore, from relative mind to Absolute Mind. As relative mind and Absolute Mind are, from the standpoint of the relative mind, absolutely discontinuous, this transition can be brought about only by means of a kind of existential leap from the one to the other. There is no longer any question of a path with clearly marked steps and stages. The path that we have so far followed ends at the brink of an abyss, and from here we have no alternative but to take a leap in the dark. Taking the leap, we find ourselves in the midst of the Void. Darkness changes to light. Suddenly and mysteriously, relative mind is replaced by Absolute Mind. This Absolute Mind is not subject as opposed to object, nor can it be itself the object of thought. Rather, it is that pure, brilliant and transparent Awareness within which the distinction of subject and object does not exist. The goal of meditation has now been reached. Reality has been 'seen'. In pointing to the mind, Zen has pointed to Reality, To Enlightenment, to Buddhahood.

Having understood what is meant by mind, and why Zen insists on pointing to the mind rather than to anything else, we come now to our third and last question: What is the significance of *direct* pointing? This is not very difficult to see. Direct pointing means referring everything back to the mind itself – referring it, in the first place, to the thinking and perceiving mind rather than to the object of its thought and perception. It means throwing the disciple back again and again on his own personal problems and his own individual resources. It means refusing to go from Hampstead to Highgate via the whole universe. The latter is, of course, just the sort of detour that people love to make. Despite protestations to the contrary, they do not really want to get to Highgate at all. They do not want to face up to the challenge of existence. They want to avoid it.

There are many ways in which this can be done. One of the most popular ways, especially in Western Buddhist circles, is by asking questions. Now you may have been thinking that people ask questions in order to dispel their doubts and clear up mental confusion and arrive at the truth, and admittedly this does sometimes happen. But most of the time people ask questions in order *not* to receive an answer. A real live answer is the last thing they want. Even if they got it they would not know what to do with it. Probably they would feel like a small boy playing at hunting lions and tigers in the garden who was suddenly confronted by a real live lion or tiger escaped from the zoo. So they go on asking questions. What is the nature of Nirvana? How can the law of Karma operate when there is no permanent self? What are the evidences for rebirth? How shall we know that we have gained Enlightenment? Where does ignorance come from? Can one really desire not to desire? How is it possible to be fully aware, when awareness means being aware that you are aware, and so on *ad infinitum*? Has a dog Buddha-nature? Why did Bodhidharma come from the West? To questions of this kind Zen gives no answer, at least it does not answer them on their own terms or from their own point of view. Generally, it prefers to put a counter-question, saying, in effect, Why do you ask the question? Or, more challengingly, Who is it that asks? In this way the exchange is at once placed on an entirely different basis. From being abstract and theoretical it becomes concrete and existential. The questioner is forced to realize, however dimly, that far from being motivated by a disinterested 'scientific' desire for the truth he is influenced by factors of which he is largely unconscious and that what he is really trying to do is to escape from the truth.

Most people, of course, resist this realization. Their own motives are the last thing they are prepared to scrutinize. But Zen does not let them get away with it so easily. By one means or another, with the help of slaps and shouts if words fail, it drags them back from philosophy and religion and psychology, even from Zen, and compels them to look where perhaps they never thought of looking before – at their own mind.

This is just what each one of you should do. Otherwise this talk will have been wasted. What I have said should be taken, however, as being itself a direct pointing to the mind. Take it as a talk *about* direct pointing to the mind, and you will miss the whole point.

Fifth Talk

Seeing into one's own nature and realizing Buddhahood.

Today we come to the fourth and last line of the traditional verse with the help of which we have been trying, during the past few weeks, to gain some insight into the essence of Zen. The line reads, 'Seeing into one's own nature and realizing Buddhahood'. The expression 'one's own nature' corresponds to the Sanskrit *svabhava*, literally 'own-being' or 'self-nature', and in this context stands for the mind on which the previous line asked us to depend. One could, therefore, also render the line as 'Seeing into one's own *mind* and realizing Buddhahood'. The word 'and', however, does not appear in the original Chinese. Indeed, I believe the Chinese language dispenses altogether with conjunctions. What one has not divided one is under no necessity of joining together again. Here the omission, as we would regard it, of the word 'and' suggests that 'seeing' into one's own nature or into one's own mind and 'realizing' Buddhahood are not two distinct, even if parallel, activities, but simply different aspects of one and the same spiritual process.

In order to understand how this process takes place let us refer to the *Surangama-samadhi Sutra*, one of the most distinguished of the great Mahayana scriptures. The scene of the Sutra is laid at Shravasti, in North-Western India, in the orchard which Anathapindika, the rich merchant, had acquired from Prince Jeta as a retreat for the Buddha. Soon after the Sutra begins the Buddha and His disciples are all invited to a great feast by the king, it being the anniversary of his father's death. At the appropriate time all therefore depart for the palace. Only Ananda, the Buddha's personal attendant, is missing. He has gone out on an errand, and returns only after the others have left. Finding the monastery deserted, and nothing to eat, he takes his almsbowl and goes begging from door to door in the streets of the city. Being a conscientious monk, he begs from all alike, without discriminating between rich and poor, or between high-caste and low-caste, and in this way eventually comes to the house of a low-caste woman called Matangi who has a beautiful daughter called Prakriti. As soon as she sees the young and handsome monk Prakriti falls violently in love with him, and begs her mother to cast a love-spell upon him. This Matangi does. Ananda, though a conscientious monk, is not proof against the assaults of magic, and not only becomes fascinated by the maiden's charms but is lured into the house and into her room.

Meanwhile, the Buddha has returned to His orchard retreat, where He discourses to the king and other notabilities, who have accompanied Him back from the palace. Knowing all the time what was happening to Ananda, however, he calls the Bodhisattva Manjushri, the embodiment of Wisdom, and bids him go and save Ananda by repeating the Great Dharani at Matangi's house. As soon as Manjushri does this, Matangi's spell loses its power, Ananda comes to his senses, and the crestfallen monk and repentant maiden accompany the great Bodhisattva back to the feet of the Buddha.

Now all this obviously has an allegorical meaning. To begin with, Matangi is a *low-caste* woman. She occupies a place, that is to say, at the very bottom of the Indian social system. Since there exists a clear correspondence between the higher and lower castes, on the one hand, and higher and lower states of consciousness, on the other, she may be said to represent the unrecognized or repressed side of one's nature. In Tantric Buddhism, indeed, the low-caste woman is the regular symbol for all the crude, unsublimated psychic energies which, according to this tradition, should not be repressed but brought out into the open and united with one's conscious spiritual attitude. It is also significant that Matangi's daughter is called Prakriti, for Prakriti means 'Nature'. Ananda is very learned and very conscientious but he is not enlightened. He has not succeeded, that is to say, in integrating the different sides of his own being. Head is still at war with heart, conscious with unconscious. The casting of the spell represents not an assault from without, but rather an attack coming from forces deep within his own unconscious mind, forces with which he has not yet come to terms. Manjushri, of course, represents Transcendental Wisdom. The conflict between head and heart, reason and emotion, conscious and unconscious mind, can be resolved only by the emergence of a higher faculty, wherein the light of reason and the warmth of emotion are not only fused but raised to the highest possible degree of intensity. Only when the Bodhisattva recites the Great Dharani does Matangi's spell lose its power. But this does not mean that the natural forces which the spell represents are simply thrust back into the darkness of the unconscious. Manjushri is no St. Michael triumphantly holding down the powers of evil. Manjushri brings Ananda back to the feet of the Buddha. But he brings Prakriti too. In other words, Nature is not to be repressed but recognized, not to be rejected but purified and assimilated.

On coming into the Buddha's presence Ananda prostrates himself before Him, confesses his shortcomings, and asks for help. The Buddha says that He will question Ananda, and that the latter should *answer spontaneously*, without recourse to discriminative thinking. The qualification is important. Ananda is a very learned man, he has 'heard much', but the Buddha does not want him to answer out of his acquired knowledge, which is after all second-hand, but out of himself, out of his personal perception and realization. He wants him to speak with his own voice, not with a borrowed voice. This sort of spontaneity is, of course, very rare. Usually, when questioned on matters of fundamental concern, we reply after much thought and deliberation. That is to say, we reply from a comparatively superficial level of our being, from one made up of accretions from without rather than creations from within, from opinion and hearsay. Only in moments of crisis, or when deeply moved, do we in a sense really speak out. It is this sort of spontaneity, only coming from even deeper, coming from the existential depth of the disciple, that the Zen *mondo* or 'exchange' between master and disciple, or between one master and another, is designed to elicit. So long as the disciple speaks from anything less than his own true mind, or Buddha-nature, the master remains unsatisfied.

Step by step, relentlessly, the disciple is therefore forced into a corner, into an impasse. All his answers rejected, his mind baffled, his intellectual resources exhausted, in a state of near collapse, he can escape from the impasse only by waking up to the reality of his own true mind, and speaking out from that, saying – whatever comes. Perhaps, indeed, what comes will not be words at all, but a laugh or a smile, a polite bow or a sudden blow. But it must be spontaneous, and it must come from the deepest possible level of his being.

It is in this manner that the Buddha wants Ananda to answer his question, and the question is, 'How did you become interested in Buddhism?' In other words the Buddha recurs to fundamentals. He does not waste time asking Ananda why he was late getting back from his errand, or why he had not kept his eyes firmly fixed on his almsbowl while begging for food at Matangi's house. Instead, like a thunderbolt out of a clear sky comes the question, 'How did you become interested in Buddhism?' As the import of the Sutra is universal and timeless, the question is addressed not only to Ananda but to us, not only to the Ananda on the stage of Buddhist history but to the Ananda in our own minds, to that aspect of ourselves which, being unintegrated, is liable, as he was liable, to the attacks of the unconscious. We too need, periodically, to explore the nature of our own commitment, to examine our reasons for following the Path to Enlightenment. Are we attracted to Buddhism by its art, or its ethics, or its metaphysics? Was it books that brought us to the feet of the Buddha or the living example of someone we know? Are we in search of psychological security? Has our Buddhist life become a matter of habit and routine? These are the sort of questions we should ask ourselves, and like Ananda we should try to answer them spontaneously.

Well, how *did* Ananda become interested in Buddhism? The answer that he gives to the Buddha's question is hardly one that it would be possible for anyone to give today. He became interested, he says, because he was impressed by the personal appearance of the Buddha, and because he was convinced that the aureole of transcendentally pure and golden brightness which he had seen emanating from His person could not originate in one who was not free from all sexual passion and desire. It was on account of this that he had admired the Buddha and it was this that had influenced him to become one of His true followers.

Approving this declaration, the Buddha then solemnly addresses the whole assembly. Sentient beings have been born and reborn since beginningless time, He tells them, because they have not realized the true Essence of Mind and its self-purifying brightness. On the contrary, they have been engrossed in deluding and transient thoughts which are nothing but falsehood and vanity, thus preparing for themselves the conditions for repeated rebirth. If Ananda is desirous of more perfectly understanding Supreme Enlightenment he must learn to answer questions spontaneously, without recourse to discriminative thinking, for it is by reliance on Their intuitive minds that the Buddhas of the ten quarters of the universe have been delivered from the cycle of conditional existence. Having said this, the Buddha asks Ananda a further question. When he saw Him, and was impressed by His appearance, how did he perceive Him?

Ananda replies that he perceived the Buddha with his eyes and his mind.

And where are these located?

The eyes, like the other sense-organs, are located on the surface of the body, while the mind is hidden within the body.

This does not satisfy the Buddha. He points out that Ananda is now sitting in the hall of the retreat. First he sees the people sitting in the hall, and other things in turn, only afterwards does he see the grove and park outside. Similarly, if Ananda's mind were hidden within his body, in the sense of being spatially located there, he ought to be able to see his own internal organs first and external objects afterwards.

Ananda tries again. The mind may, after all, be located outside the body. It may be like a lamp which would illuminate the inside of the room first and then, shining through the doors and windows, illuminate the yard outside.

This, too, fails to satisfy the Buddha. One person's eating does not appease the hunger of all. In the same way, if Ananda's perceiving, understanding mind is really outside his body, then what the mind perceives could not be felt by the body, and what the body feels could not be perceived by the mind. Mind and body are in mutual correspondence, as is proved by the fact that when Ananda's eyes are looking at the Buddha's hand his mind makes discriminations about it. If mind and body are in mutual correspondence, it cannot possibly be said that the mind exists outside the body.

Ananda still thinks the mind must be located somewhere. If it cannot exist either inside or outside the body it must be located somewhere in between. Indeed, it may be concealed within the sense-organ itself. Just as the eye may be covered with a crystal bowl, so the mind may be 'covered' by, or contained within, the eye. Being part of the eye it cannot see the inside of the body, but being concealed within the eye it can clearly perceive external objects.

To this explanation the Buddha objects that if the mind were, in fact, contained within the eye as the eye itself might be covered by a crystal bowl, then the mind ought to perceive the eye before perceiving external objects, just as the eye would see the bowl before seeing mountains and rivers.

In this way the dialogue proceeds. Ananda and the other members of the great assembly eventually realize that the mind, not being a spatially conditioned phenomenon, cannot be located anywhere. There is no time to follow the argument in detail, as step by step the Buddha leads Ananda to the highest realization, but it should already have become evident that the *Surangama-samadhi Sutra* is one of the most magnificent of all Buddhist dialogues. Rivalling even Plato in atmosphere and in beauty of setting, its content is even profounder, being nothing else than the progressive revelation of the Buddha's Crowning Experience, His experience of the Highest Samadhi.

Now the mind not only cannot be located anywhere, but it does not exist as a thing among things at all. Not being a thing, an object, it cannot really be perceived or seen. But the fourth line of our verse, the line with which we are at present dealing, speaks of seeing into one's own nature, that is to say, into one's mind. Obviously there is a contradiction here. How is it to be resolved?

This brings us to one of the profoundest and most important teachings of Mahayana Buddhism, to a teaching of which Zen, at its best, is simply a practical exemplification. *One sees the mind by not seeing.* Not being an object of perception but the principle of perception itself, the mind cannot ever be perceived. Whatever is perceived is not the mind. For the mind to try to perceive its own existence is therefore like the tip of the finger trying to touch itself. Whatever is touched is not the finger-tip. The only way in which the finger-tip can possibly 'touch' itself is by withdrawing from all contact with external objects and simply 'feeling' its own existence directly. Similarly with the mind. We can never know it by going after it – with the mind – as though it were an external object distinct from the mind. This is what Zen calls "using the mind to seek for the mind" and it is quite useless. By following this procedure, we may discover many 'minds', but we shall not be able to discover the true mind, the principle of perception itself. The true mind can be found only by not-finding, by the realization, that is to say, of a pure non-dual Awareness without distinction of subject and object.

What has been said about 'seeing one's own mind' applies with equal force to 'realizing Buddhahood', for, as we have already seen, the two are different aspects of the same process. 'Seeing' corresponds to 'realizing', 'Mind' to 'Buddha'. Just as it is ridiculous for the mind to try to see the mind, so it is ridiculous for the mind to try to realize Buddhahood. Zen tells us: You are Buddha. All that we have to do, it declares, is to wake up to the significance of this supreme fact. Devotional practices, scriptural study, even meditation, are ultimately a waste of time. Engaging in them is "using the Buddha to realize the Buddha", which is like a man's going in search of himself.

Of course it is not so easy to wake up. In fact it requires a great deal of effort to do so. First of all we have to realize, however vaguely, that we are asleep. As you sit here listening to these words you are not awake, as perhaps you had imagined, but asleep, sound asleep. Zen is simply a voice crying "Wake up! Wake up!" Loud and clear though it resounds in your ear, so deep are your slumbers that you hear it but faintly, and coming as it were from a great distance. For five weeks now I have been talking about Zen; yet no one seems to have woken up. Perhaps I have not yet woken up myself. Perhaps I have just been talking in my sleep all this while. However, it sometimes happens that by talking in his sleep one sleeping person may rouse another. Let us hope that as a result of these talks on the Essence of Zen something of that nature might have occurred.